T0156575

Moon Shell

by G. Julian Walker

authorHOUSE®

AuthorHouse™
1663 Liberty Drive
Bloomington, IN 47403
www.authorhouse.com
Phone: 1-800-839-8640

Published by AuthorHouse   03/22/2012

ISBN: 978-1-4685-4000-0 (sc)

Contents

Invocation: prayer for the lost dream

To the person

Who could have been a parson +
To the actor—live wire
Who wanted to be a cab-driva
Or who went wild
Over Lady Godiva
>   *I am speaking pal*
>   *Of your lost dream gal*

The one that always
Comes close (near Miss)
Of Poets & Poems—only a notion
Of masterpieces muff-ed
On bad association,
Dreams postponed from
Unwanted situations
Charity cases without End:
Lord grant me my true worth
My karma mend.

"By giving the common a noble meaning,
the ordinary a mysterious aspect, the known
the dignity of the unknown, the finite the
appearance of the infinite—I Romanticise."
Novalis

1.   Perfumes of the Morning

Columbian Coffee Comes
Drifting it's brewing aroma
The incense of orange orange
Is followed by bandana banana
Brahms gently breaks
And spotlights of sunbeams
Beckon from the blue

All the spice and nutmeg
Of cardamom & cinnamon stick
Macadamian & walnut

With nosehair as teeth
My Mind opens to
Spiritual flavors

The window cracks:
Let it out
Let it out
It is my offering
To . . . The Lord of the Sky . . . .

1

2.   A Rich Woman's Breakfast

Something in my mind
        likes a quiet place
                a tender face
        and a rose so rare

a border of white lace
and a taste beyond come pear
Here's a toast
and bread and butter too
with sweet me in bed.

A magnificent view
is flooded with light
as swaying curtains
waft subtle perfumes

On this day
the blue jay
sings yet another song
the butterfly seems to say
"O Day of Sun,
through the night
a miracle won,
though many were forlorn
many were being born."

A clear view of the meadow
moves with the mild may breezes
My Reverie is Renewed
as a gold star
glimmers from the tea urn.

Something in me
likes a quiet place
Reawaken to a gentle face
take a fragrant taste
a flower, a loving smile
and a reflection so rare
that we are born daily
with satsuma as sustenance.

3.   Menu

Early in the Morning
i arose
bemused and foggy
I saw
> through the kitchen door
> a chore undone
> a glass of milk; a bun
> a piece of fruit
> and a letter in red, unread

A few years later
i visited a museum
i looked at a canvas
amused and soggy
i saw
> through the kitchen door
> a chore undone
> a glass of milk; a bun
> a piece of fruit
> and a telegram unread.

Later than that
i remember
confused and groggy
at a party dancing
            through the kitchen door
            found . . . . on the floor; a chore
            a glass of beer—to boot—
            a piece of fruit and
            war in the newspaper unread

4. The Trumpet Call

The trumpet call has sounded
    Above the tops of trees
I, from my bed have floundered
    And fallen to my knees
The smell of sweet flowers
    Is on the drift
And into my window
    Comes a strange colored mist
Birds gather and sing a chorus
Butterflies come out of the forest

A tree limb knocks
    Upon my window pane
"Come Out!" says the circus
    "Do-not Disdain!"
I clothe myself
    And run astride . . .
The music of Spring
    Comes in like the tide
Trombones and Trumpets
    I have heard on high
Outside—I find:
    the quietest blue lake
and, the clearest blue sky.

5. Stat Yam Recipe

Start by stirring Spicy Chutney
Suie—Guie, Rat Sahib
Too Much
Too much Rasberry
Too much Jam
Get Rhythm
Get Style
Smack Jack
Jam-a-Jackarat
Add warm Panamanian nights
With hats and bands of
Tropical Sunshine
Elephant Ears drip dew drops
        A breath of mantra
        a touch of tantra

Alas: Dragon Brew Broth Boils
                Take,

                        Take,

                One loyal Dogflea

6.   White Moccasins

Raindrops dripped
   Tree limbs drupped
The Storm of Night
   Still charged the air

I breathe the new air, so clean and sweet
And walk through the woods—in a dream
The branches swish as I pass the green
Scent to my nose, water on my feet

As I come up the hill
The Lake below is still
Across the shore
In strangest shadow
A Rainbow over Woodland's Door

I close my eyes
      still drowsy with sleep
A Feeling of wonder
      Came up from the deep
Suddenly Opening
      my eyes with a Shake
A Strange Shimmering
      Came over the Lake
Softly but bold
      a girl tiptoed
White moccasins were on her feet!

7.   Cummings Skwyway

Full Moon Magnolis Bloom upon this Isle
mixing their fragrance with Strange Shadows tall
Oh kiss this Sacred Lake in Summer Season,
While another dimension arises with Magical Call:
        Come Away, Come Away with me!

A better source of water, the legend goes
Flows . . . from the Lake of Miracles,
Healing and Revealing:
        The Land of the Sky Blue Water.

Thusly I reflect as a good listener
with the gleaming warm glow of the Lake
and it's fearful whisper:
       Come Away, Come Away with me!

I cup my hands with moonlit fingers
and drink the nectar without fear
Dull Diamond Moons glitter/glimmer in the water
falling through swan-like fingers clear

and still it seems
among the aqua and green
Shapes deep within appear
it's crystalline color uneasily near
        Come to the Land of the Sky Blue Water!

Here is this feelin' that's showin'
that all my life's been growin'
Methinks it's my Lord with low moan
Inviting me cordially to Come Home
with whispering sighs—o—I heard Him Say
        Come, Come . . . . in the sky away!

The Cosmic Romantic is a special meditation:
he is sentimental about the Supreme Lord.

8.   Sacred Sunday

Amongst the Sequoias
Grand and Imposing
A Band of naked bandits
descended down to
      the Hot Springs
          Pool.

Large Slithers of Gold
      tonsured their heads,
Guilt glimmered off
      their eyes
As their minds reminisce
      in the mist
         of church
            not attended.

Being Nudely Inspired
I arose with a Splash! ~
      and greeted their conscience:

Welcome to the Cathedral
      I am the Pastor:
         Mr. Natural

9.   The Psychic Communicator

The Sun Sent Beacons of Glory
         shading in shadow the tops of trees
Another day entered the log
Arising from the Mists of Morn
Friendly Ghosts Come Up to Greet me
The Hot Springs hidden in the wilderness
Offered a Summer of Rest & Recuperation.

         The fog blew away
and Lovely, lounging Mermaids
were revealed on the Rocks
         Streamlined museles gleam with Sweat
I press my ear close to the Hot Falls
. . . . and hear the gurgling and croaking of subtle
frogs
I look away and watch the Enchanted Forest.

Suddenly my Third Eye is Glowing and
An Organ Choral Hymn Comes Droning down.
I Rise upon a smooth rock
and Spirits Dance Tai-Chi with me
Emerging from the Cold Waterfall
is a Joyful Splashing Renaissance.

Purification Being the Principle
I am ready for the world.
Clothed and Preened I walk away

Behind me—The Presiding Deity Appears:
A Shimmering Ravishing Goddess
who blows me a kiss and
whispers an affectionate goodbye
            on the Astral Byways.

10. Poem Before the Storm

Brilliant Before the Sun
vibrant and vibrating
in hot resilient silt,
We bake and shine
with naked behind,
Can you hear how my heart beats True?

Suddenly Blown
from Coverall Breezes
A-Blowing of clouds—
and Blistering of Trees
        Come Dark Battalions
        Armies of Clouds
        With Breath ,Cool
Hurrying—Mean-Cold & Wild!
A Storm is Coming
A Storm is Coming, Mad!!
Can you hear how my heart beats True?

I want this fresh Breeze-this fierce zephyr
Frantically blowing on my sun burnt face
It calls Forth Miracles of Purple Fury
Wet and Wild-it stings my brow
Now is the time to ask the World:
Does my heart beat True?

Flashing Lightning Strikes Here *~Crack!!!
       I feel it++ I feel it++
My Heart Does Beat True!

11. Romantic Raindrops

A woman should add dignity
Thought the gent w/top hat tall
A man should add dignity
Thought the miss w/ evening dress and all

White shining gloves pointed
    Up to a charcoal sky
"Hurry before the incoming storm
soaks all our fine clothes."

Fickle remorse &reaction from the past
Haunted her memory and then alas
It gathered black momentum
Like the incoming storm;
    It was born

Oh woe to the one who is so blind
To see no need to control the mind
Yea, the evil thought came sprinkling down;
The gentleman was irked but without a sound
A lightning glance of anger came around
She as his mate added the thunder
And thus they began to wonder:
      Shouldn't a woman add dignity
Thought the man going away
      Shouldn't a man add dignity
Thought the lady abandoned by the way.

It was a cold and cruel night of regret
Violence echoed across the sky
Hatred floated on a flash:
      Somewhere the light must be burning bright
but for this pair-hot tears were elected to mix
With cold rain/undetected.

12. Gambling Fever

"I have a dream" King   "you had one too" Ragtime

The Soloist felt ill   coming onstage to an
ocean of applause

One million microwave   commuters can't be wrong
Standing on their ears   singing the Anvil Chorus

"Go to Hell and Fry!"   smiled the cop in court
"Do-not Pass Go!"   stammered the judge.

May I collect $200   pleaded a victim
from his souped up   wheel-chair

Monotony Maddens   the Masses
Muddles the Misses   and a P Pals the Palette

"Oh please!"   pleaded Pinocchio
to the tiny fairy   "let Cinderella get married
in Reno!

"you buzzed!"   grinned the grinding dentist

Then the surgeon with scalpel in hand
wanted to scalp me with his golden plan

"Take a chance life is a tightrope of
romance."

Alas, I reached into my dream
And grabbed the blue video fruit!
Please God release the money!

Bells Began to Blare Balloons Began to Bulge
Busty Beauties Began to kiss me* * *
Siren and flashing lights blinded me
As Outside, it snowed ticker tape
The Casino Manager and the Devil appeared
As they offered double or nothing

Two former millionaires jumped off the Golden
Gate
Their Desperate Plea: We have the most complete
poverty

13. Prison Ballard Blues =

I was dreaming the life of mediocrity
When, with cold hand and angry pall
    I had a fall:
          "Clang!" went the incrimination
          Faces I saw were mean
          Aghast, I saw another scene.

"Welcome to Life's zero!
          said a one-eyed Jack
"Dark Tidings!"
          whispered the ace of Spades
Condemned to cold, concrete days
and forgotten in nights of drab,
          "We Kiss Away"
          "We Piss Away"
Upon this our crowded mount
veiled & weary eyes are down for the count.

We hailed the karma kar
that railroaded us in,
Looked down the trac-a-lack
and prayed to the conductor
for a 2-way ticket back.

14. Earthquake Madness

They're coming to take me away, ha-ha!
They're coming to take me away!
With a hey, dilly-dilly dill
I am taken against my will
With a hey, dilly-dilly day
I'm taken away from the Bay.

I will surely be zapped on Zappa
or dreaming of napping in Napa
When presently, I'll be jolted!?
Hey, the ground needs to be bolted!!
Without paying to be ferried
We will all be merrily buried
a gay opera chorus shrill
will accompany us downhill
All my friends underground will be singing
or why is the phone in my head still ringing?

Don't you dare, dare worry
Dear Debra, Dorris & Murray
The topsoil folks will supply the sediment
The shaky Bedrock is the only impediment.
That's why, with a hey,
They're coming to take me away
To make me the blooming President
of the whole damn-fall

            i

              n

                g

                    Settlement.

15. The Prophet

Wizard with Ball
Suit   and   tie

Flowing Robes in the Wind "" ""
                perfumes fly

Magic Wand %
Magic Carpet   =====
(Rubies are Raining) *****

Look! Look! Into the Future ^
        See the Miracles There +++
                Where!? @ (_____)
Throw in the Hair ##""
Coated . . . .   With   Pollinated
Pellets
The Feather Floats
        From

                Mystic

                Fires. ("" "")

16. Hymn to the Bohemian

In the Dark
by eerie canals of erie
Came a fellow
a jester
a clown
a magician
for the King
from the Sorcerer

A Bearer of Wealth
unending stealth
and the double ended
blessings of Laxmi/Nishringha

Pictures and Prizes
appealing to the eyes
A Love into heil
he brought me a smile

A hint into print
a painting he sent
greetings from God
It was He that penned it
O Blessed New World
        with Friendship   init.

17. Blind Trust

Yin to Strong for Yang?
Mellow out with me
        Mellow tea!
Ohm mau mau
Ohnm mau mau
Kappa Kappa
Gamma Gamma
Omega! Omega!

18. Hindu Festival

All of Mankind at large
      is invited to a party!
It will be held on the wing
Outside
      on the first day of Spring
      We will gladly   Sing:

Goura—Purnima Hey!
We'll celebrate that day ***

In the sunshine gold
Chanting—Brother & Sister
Nitie-Gouranga, Hare Krishna

At night, in sacred tunic
we'll croon, in downtown Munich
Under the watchful eye of Balaram
In the full bloom of Moon
We will chant and nod
A candlelight cakewalk   with
      Shri-Ishopanishad.

19. Poet meets Poet

Howdoyoudo? O.K. a little blue
        (He didn't mention
        the pain in his arm
        subluxation of the spine
        I could die and not know why!?

Anythingnewithyou? Nothing new, it's true
        (He didn't mention
        how he stayed awake all night
        staring in shock at the shadow
        of a Monster on his kitchen wall:
        which turned out to be a
        Bonsai Tree-Top the fridge
        growing out of a fruit cake!?

Well Man, Tell ya' bout it later.
I'm sure you will, you instigator!!

20. The Good Fairy of Poets

You are patiently wading through a reading
at your one-thousandth marathon poetry reading
It's a 5-hour Olympian Feat
        of 500 poets in - heat:
                Reader after Reader
                    is Time Burglar
                        or Word Juggler

You have endured this scene of sophistry milling
        derelicts cussing, sermons, and political spleen
                and rhyme dentistry drilling
You wonder whether it's wrong to be a mole
for your mind wants to crawl into a hole.

When suddenly, as if the Lord heard your prayer
Everyone's hair shot straight up in the air:
An inspired chick in the rear-whispered something about
free beer
A stampede of ostriches ran over my chair.

They laughed and sang a chorus
and promised never more to bore us

dancing out came a queen = in drag
waving a wand as part of his bag
said he, waving around his stick
"I'm gonna show ya (hick) ma magic trick
    Just on account of—all your good looks
        I'm a-gonna publish all your books!"

21. O Education O

Stop, Look   and Listen
Berkeley   incline thine ear
          -Ye glass blowers
Pause   for the elevator
Really does stop—atop—Campanile

Believe thou me:
          Mine eyes have seen the glory
                    Of the coming of the coeds
Particularly, the brand of marriageable
          Nymphs *** which are armed
                    With large breasts
                              Legs luscious
Long hair and ruby lips
          (Beware the voice of the Bedeker Mother
          (Oh Brother, Kodak eyes are everywhere
               at night   there are barely seven
          Grand & Royal
          I am   Loyal   to the Stars of Heaven

22. Low Profile

Tiptoeing through the thicket
    a camouflaged man comes
       he crouches and waits
          a crotchety old man
            silent and alone
               he sits alone at sunset.

He watches a deer
    casually stride past
       he says . . . nothing
        he is not noticed.

His eyes alone peer
    from the forest
       his only prayer
        is that
           the Lord of Death
              will not find him there.

23. Death in July

The crowds were roaring with delight
it was the floats, the flowers, the sights:
The sky a-blueing
The weather a-wooing
        suddenly—I died.

The movie reel parade
clacked and burned the film
faces with stunned amazement
        award the prize.

The baton with the big band sound
fell lifeless to the ground
The Wind Wafted the Flowers Again

The Bandmaster rallied
and with inspiration filling
Cried: Your Spirit & Joy Renew
        Precious Summer is
        Only for the living.

*The Neo-Romantic Poet celebrates life as
an adventure, a study and a meditation.*

24. May Night in Moonlight

Cruising by in distant waves
a breeze of light—I hail
across the grass
Oho—go the Roses in Blue
My Sail has taken to the Wind
My Soul flies the Romantic Flag

A furious flurry has landed
like an alien light show
with astral projection showing
The snows of Kilimanjaro

What else has been transported
Sages & Gods
Ghosts and Sprites
Not even a whisper is reported.

Himalayan Snowstorm
has lashed 'cross the eye line:
such cooling, soothing rays
you never will find.

It entered my garden
like a brocaded velvet suit
shimmering paint 'cross the carpet
driping from the cup of life
       Nectarine Carnamrita
       Creme' de la Creme
       Keech & Tulsi Crepe

Oh no
The snows of Kilimanjaro
were never like this!
Methinks the invisible s n o w m a n
has unlimited white Reindeer
their sweet, dark kisses turn me on
Because they are softer than Teddy Bears
And huggable ~ right here ~ on the chocolate lawn.

25. *Nocturnal Banquet*

I sometimes awake
late at night with hunger
looking up in the dark
with a black sky for tablecloth
I Spy, a vanilla moon pie
and birthday candles burning yonder
But my starry eyed dreaming
of just one bite
makes me drowsy and jaded
so I return to the night

It was a fort night later
that I awoke with a smart
a hunger burned inside me
even deep in the dark
Looking up startled
alarming I found
a half-eaten moon
and crumbs on the ground
Who has taken this
gigantic late night snack?

Glancing up again
i as of luck did find
the cosmological hunter
preparing again to dine:
      a glowing crumb
            fell from his
                 invisible mouth
                     divine.

26. I Am An Ancient Egyptian Mummy

My hands are crossed
My mind is embossed
Occasionally, I smell
My home—a comfortable cell
Has golden corridors with secret print

Sometimes I feel so peaceful
Hovering over my body
Looking down—at the mound
Of gold & emerald booty
(my toys—all dusty & sooty)

Posted on the walls
Are guidelines for my guests
        No coughing or cussing
        in the Sarcophicus

One eye looks upward
One eye looks inward
Every century an ultrasonic alarm++
Whines Long & Hearty

My ghost attendants come then
For my birthday party
They bring silks & moldy cake
It is then that purple perfumes rise
And fog cloaks my home—in disguise

Hookahs go 'round with Hash
As everyone does the Monster Mash
When the Zombies dance & shake
We all sing Hare Krishna and play Tag
          to the tune of the Magnetic   Rag!

27. The Universal Chasm

Knocked out of orbit and
hanging on only Stardust
I am a mystic moon
Life is guaranteed with a smile
While my brother
      arrived by Starchip
            from the Andromeda Galaxy

I retripped
      the Anti-Matter
         Zen Robitron
My new Destination
Twin Blue Stars in the Horsehead Nebula
With a Rainbow Road to walk on
My Sincere Inquiry Remains
Are you, Reader++ Reading
      From = ? a parallel universe - upside down

28. The Whirlpool

A ring of leaves
        goes whirling around
they skip and whisper low:
        The Wind is blowing
and throwing something up
        and up and up and
around in a circle of sound
Like a Whirlpool—at sea
        Your ship is looking down
at certain destruction swirling 'round
Rotating darkly below == like a black hole
And now the Winter Sky
        in looming above us
            It seems to know: how to grow

Ominously, it looks down threatningly
        a feeling is coming
            of gloomy Ar-ma-geddon - 0 -

29. Something in the Wind

White and dark animals
rush to ongoing seasons
stark and bold forebodings

There is a stormy symphony brewing
A keen edge on the wind says:
        cold ahead so be
                cool, play it—real cool

The sun bounced off the clear wavelets
        of glaciated lake
                carrying the breeze
                        the tease and
                                elation:
An invitation + to one more swim*

The sun came down to a deeper setting
Thank you Lord, for small favors
        and small waterfalls

A River that was once
        clear and strong—is now
            soft and slow:

Floating on it's amber clarity
        Yellow Leaves
            Leaves of Change.

30. The Troubled Musicians
(Dedicated to Michael Smith of the Netherlands)

Gone are the Summer Breezes

that made his Idyl Smile

Gone are the Sunshine Beacons

that sent energy Bands a—while

Autumn stopped us cold

and the musicians prepared to play

Furrowed brows signaled their worry

The Strings loose their stops

The Reeds loose their sharps

Their brooding melody of flats

Speaks of meditation

The orchestra hints darkly of a

       Stormy Symphony

31. Avant Garde Haiku

the hour swims
            beyond time
before sunrise

faces at night
eulogies by firelight
sparks fly upward

black clouds move
animals look down
autumn looks angry

eyes open
warm sun smiles
breezes blow kisses
Waterfall laughs

32. Abstract Poem

This poem has no meaning
       I repeat . . . no meaning
It is like the lonely one
       Toward love leaning
Resplendent in spiritual color
       Toward a great abstraction

       Teaming

It also has no visible lover

33. Moon Shell

Found on a bright moon night
amidst the glitter of sand
When a cloud of iridescent mist
moved down from the Gods

Oh vapor of iridescent mist
by your moving
you have completely confused my mind
Oh black hole all creamy
may I enter your world?

As I was thus singing
the nocturnal song of Spring
a slime of silver-gray captured me
            and I shrunk into a pea-pearl
                    i slept glistening
and was found the next morning
as a decoration on your vanity

33 & 1/3

The Transcendental Bedtime Prayer

Now I lay my body down—for sleeping

My Soul, Lord Hari, is in your keeping

If I should die before I awake

I request Vishnu-dutas—My Soul to Take

And if I'm worthy, thus to speak:

I pray you Lord, that at last—we meet!